Joyful Jenna

KELSEY KIRK

ISBN: Softcover   978-1-5434-4142-0
        Hardcover   978-1-5434-4141-3
        EBook   978-1-5434-4143-7

Print information available on the last page

Rev. date: 08/01/2017

To order additional copies of this book, contact:
Xlibris
1-888-795-4274
www.Xlibris.com
Orders@Xlibris.com

Joyful Jenna

KELSEY KIRK

Joyful Jenna has a joyful sound, and people should come from miles around to hear her song, to hear her voice, and soon they would find they made a wondrous choice!

But there is a secret she holds so dear. She doesn't dare to share for fear of someone thinking she was oh so wimpy, so she keeps it hidden. It's done so simply.

For Jenna has been told for years, she has this special gift. A token from God, her parents said, that can give peoples' hearts a lift. And even though she knows this fact, she can't seem to be brave, to share this wonderful love of song that God so generously gave.

For in her dreams, she has this vision of people enjoying her song. Her belting out note after note, and everyone applauding along. But in reality, no one knows what she has. In her awakened world she hides, and she only lets her voice sing out when only her loved ones abide.

And then one day, there came a whisper inside her ear so soft that only Joyful Jenna could hear where her memories and thoughts lie aloft. This voice was God's angel so heavenly and bright, telling Joyful Jenna to show God's light.

12

Use this gift God gave in her heart to show others that He is the place to start. The place to start a new life through Christ. The place where all troubles were dealt with one sacrifice. This was her way, if not by any other, to share her joyful voice with fellow sisters and brothers.

So she rose from her pew, and slowly she walked, with trembling knees and head slightly docked.

She gave her parents
one last wink, and tears
in their eyes, they knew
what to think. Here it
comes. Here it is. We've
been waiting and praying
for everyone to see what's
been hiding and laying.

18

And oh, that sound that came from her voice was a sound unheard of, and God's angel rejoiced. For now the pews would be filled with wondrous believers as they see little Joyful Jenna sharing songs about our redeemer!

And just like in her dreams, people now enjoy her song. She belts out note after note and everyone applauds along. And just like in her dreams, Joyful Jenna makes a joyful sound. Now people come from miles around, to hear her song, to hear her voice, and soon they find they made a wondrous choice!

Printed in the United States
By Bookmasters